CONCEIVE
BELIEVE
ACHIEVE

DAVID IMONITIE

Conceive, Believe, Achieve is published under Mission books, sectionalized division under Di Angelo Publications INC.

MISSION BOOKS

an imprint of Di Angelo Publications Conceive, Believe, Achieve. Copyright 2020 Di Angelo Publications in digital and print distribution in the United States of America.

Di Angelo Publications 4265 San Felipe St. #1100
Houston, Texas, 77027 www.diangelopublications.com

Library of congress cataloging-in-publications data

Conceive, Believe, Achieve. Downloadable via Kindle, iBooks and NOOK.

Library of Congress Registration Hardback

ISBN-13: 978-1942549581

Original text: David Imonitie Cover: Savina Deianova Layout: Di Angelo Publications Developmental Editor: Elizabeth Geeslin Zinn Editors: Kim James and Erin Larson

1.   Non-fiction

2.   Non-fiction——Biography——Business——United States of America with int. Distribution.

DEDICATION

This book is dedicated to my mother for teaching me and raising me to believe in God, to believe in myself, and to believe in people.

"Having a definition of purpose is the most important tool you must have to accomplish your dreams and goals."

-David Imonitie

TABLE OF CONTENTS

CHAPTER 1

MY STORY

In the world of network marketing, there are many people that join in and get started. There are some people who do not go through the journey to the point where they reach their desired destination in life. I was one of those people. I got started in the business about seven years ago.

I went through a journey, but things weren't working out like I thought they would and I was not getting what I wanted. Then something happened. It was like a magical thing that suddenly occurred after four years of struggling. All of a sudden, things started to go in a different direction for me. From that moment of sudden change until today, the transformation has been amazingly powerful.

Before the transition I went through, I was absolutely broke. I was living with my father. I was sleeping on a twin bed and I had no money. Today, upon the writing of this book which I began about two and a half years after I changed, money is not a problem. I am generating multiple six figures every single month – multiple seven figures per year. And now you're going to get a chance to hear a little more about my story. I've been listening to my mentor's audio lectures for years and now my own story being shared!

There are a few basic concepts that allowed me to be able to pull off my success and that's what I'm going to share with you. What you will read here is simple, but it isn't easy—and it isn't for those who aren't willing to do whatever it takes to make it happen.

WHAT YOU WILL READ HERE IS SIMPLE ...

BUT IT ISN'T EASY.

AND IT ISN'T FOR THOSE WHO AREN'T WILLING TO DO WHATEVER IT TAKES TO MAKE IT HAPPEN.

Conceive, Believe, Achieve

Going back to the very beginning, at a very young age mom told me to do all the things that I'm sure many mothers and other caregivers tell their children—go to school, get good grades, graduate and reap all the benefits we're told we'll get if we follow that path. I tried that. I started off in Kindergarten as all children typically do. I performed well in primary and elementary school. When I graduated from high school, my mom insisted that I go to college and I attended a university for four years.

I had 32 credits after four years of schooling! I didn't go to class and eventually I dropped out of college. I was then introduced to the industry of network marketing at the age of 21. In the beginning, I didn't have any success. I was with that company for two years and struggled terribly that entire time. However, I learned a lot of important lessons and met some good people. I stepped away from networking for about six months. I spent some time coaching tennis with my dad.

My Story

I was still living with my dad at that time that I was reintroduced to the industry and the juices really started flowing again. I became involved with another company and failed with that company. I spent two years and four months working with that company.

During that time, I learned even more. I was given a chance to meet a mentor of mine who changed everything for me. We met in 2007 and that was when the magic really began to transpire. It was then that I actually had a clear picture of what could possibly happen with network marketing. To look back on where I was when I first began writing this book—living with my father and sleeping on a twin sized bed and only having a thousand dollars to my name to now—so much has changed.

These changes are not just outward in appearance with materialistic things such as cars, houses and clothes. I also changed internally ... my whole mentality shifted. I have become a multi-millionaire with the opportunities that were presented to me and it has been incredible, but what is even more incredible is that we all possess what it takes to reach our desired goals.

Chapter 2

THE NETWORK MARKETING INDUSTRY

So, what was it about the industry that got me excited in the first place? What made me say, "You know what, I want to do that, I *really* want to do that." Did I think it would be easier than it was?

The truth is that I really didn't have a choice except to make it work. I love the concept of really being able to help people get what they want out of life. I love the concept of being able to show people that it doesn't matter what your background is, it doesn't matter where you're from, it doesn't matter your race, your creed—anything like that. You can actually get involved in something, start it from scratch and work your way all the way to the top. This is what I love about the network marketing industry.

Corporate America really doesn't allow you to do that. If you're going to get to the top it's going to take you 20 – 30 years. I read in a book during my first year of network marketing that if you survive in the network marketing for 10 years, you'll be wealthy beyond your wildest imagination.

The word survive stuck out to me—that gives the impression that there's going to be a fight. So I told myself, "Well, let me get ready for the fight," and for me it took four and a half years to find that survival breakthrough. Once I found that breakthrough, it became all about helping other people understand that there is a process that they're going to have

IT
DOESN'T
MATTER
WHAT YOUR
BACKGROUND IS.

IT DOESN'T
MATTER
WHERE YOU'RE
FROM.

to go through and *grow* through and that it is going to allow them to get to where it is that they want to go. We become excited about what's happened, but then we become even more excited about what's about to take place.

CHAPTER 3

PICTURE THE END RESULT!

What allowed me to keep pressing forward, to stay in the game, to move forward, even though things weren't happening for me immediately, is that I learned what I now teach—that you must *begin* with the *end* in mind. I had a clear picture of what the end result already looked like. The things that I had to go through in the interim didn't matter. I remember driving from Houston to Baton Rouge, a five-hour ride, and not even having a hotel room; having to sleep in my car after giving a meeting—after talking to a couple hundred people about the opportunities they could have. They dropped me back off at the hotel and said goodbye to me at the lobby. And as soon as they drove off, I would go back to my car and sleep there. I slept in my car multiple times, but it was only because I had a clear picture of what the end result looked like. I was already there. In my mind, I already saw myself as a multi-millionaire. I already saw myself with all the things that are happening today; I saw it back then. You look at that word SAW – I saw it. Look at the word backwards – WAS – I was already there. I was already living that type of lifestyle in my mind. It was just waiting for the physical equivalent to actually take place.

It is key to be in the right environment. I was in the right environment even though I failed in those companies. I was around other people who were successful—people like Emmanuel Bernstein who was one of my very first mentors. I got a chance to meet him when I was 21 years old. At that time, he was earning a multiple five figure a month income. Once again, I had a clear picture of what really could look like—the end result of it. When you have the right environment, you have the right people around you making sure that you're listening to the correct information. I grew up listening to people like Tony Robbins, listening to people like my host here, my mentor, and so many other leaders such as Les Brown. I was always listening to that information. One of the very first books that I ever read was *Think and Grow Rich* by Napoleon Hill. Reading that book and understanding that thoughts are things was imperative. I said to myself, "If I want to change things in my life, I'm going to have to change the thoughts in my life." And I really started to study that, started to really listen deeply, and read more often. I believe that all the information that I actually listened to is what allowed me to be here today.

That's a common trend of all leaders in this industry. They do see the end in the very beginning before they even start. SAW—I WAS it! That's really powerful. I actually did something that Jim Rohn teaches. He says that whenever things are not going well or you're not where you want to be, you can borrow from the vision of the future, or borrow from the promise of the future, which will allow you to engage in activities today. What this means —borrowing from vision in the future — is not as complicated as it may sound. It is simply envisioning exaclty where you want to be and then feeling what you would feel if it were to be true. You have to act like it is true! Try it with something small to test it. See yourself buying something you'd like that you feel is attainable, and imagine the feeling of the purchase and walking out of the door with your bag in hand. What does it feel like? Where is your mind at that moment? Feel it to be true. Test it. Once you see that it works on smaller things for you, you can do the same thing for larger goals.

There's a formula that I came up with: desire + skills x faith = success. You must have that burning desire. I believe that's the beginning. That's the genesis of everything that we're going to talk about. Everything that you're going to do is going to be wrapped around what your burning desire is. What's your magnificent obsession that you have? Once you know what you want, you've got to add the skills. In the four and a half years of being with those companies, all I was doing was adding the skills—the skills of knowing how to interact with people, learning how to give a presentation, understanding how to prospect, knowing how to do all the things that are necessary for one to become successful in this industry. I needed to give myself time to really understand. Most people want to get in and make a million dollars the next day. Well, it doesn't work like that. You've got a desire to make a million dollars. That's great! But now let's add the skills of a millionaire. And then multiply that by faith.

Faith comes by listening and hearing. The more often that I heard it over and over and over again and saying it to myself, the auto-suggestion, the more the faith was ingrained in me and my subconscious. Saying it to myself over and over and over again—repeating it, having it on index cards, having it on signs everywhere where I could actually see the end result led to the success that we've had today. But you've got to continue it—even after becoming a multimillionaire. Even after a little bit of success. Maybe you start earning $10,000 a month, $20,000 a month; you still better stay on that path of desire. The path of desire plus skills in this book multiplied by faith equals the success that you are looking for.

Now when it comes to skill, we would assume that everyone who is listening to or reading this information right now most likely has the desire or else they probably wouldn't be reading this. But once again, the necessary ingredient is that magnificent obsession. Speaking in the language of Napoleon Hill and W. Clement Stone—that's what they talk about. Let us say that someone is really hungry as Les Brown explains they really want to make this happen in a big way, deep down inside. Now it is time to bring in the skill. Let us say that a person starts learning the skills that are going to be required. They've got to learn how to attract people to their reality and learn how to convert once they attract these people to their reality. They want to learn how to retain people once they get them started and they want to learn how to develop leaders. All of these are different types of skills.

Even though it wasn't initially working for me, I never ever doubted that it was going to work. I could *see* that it worked. There was clear evidence around me that it was working for others and I just knew that it would work in time for me. And that's the key thing that everybody has to understand. It does work in time, but you've got to be persistent. You've got to be persistent with everything that you're doing and understand that the end result is going to take place. It has no choice but to happen. But most people quit before the end result manifests. Thus, persistence is really the seed for faith. If I know that it is going to happen and I believe it's going to happen, then I'll continue to go down that path. I'll continue to do whatever it is that I have to do and learn whatever it is that I have to learn.

CHAPTER 4

HAVE A MENTOR
OR A COACH

Mentoring is a cornerstone in developing your desire into your reality. Having a coach, having somebody that you can actually call on, having somebody that you can actually watch, is invaluable.

I learned something very important from Jeff Olsen, who teaches about the four different types of knowledge, which are also the four types of learning styles: Learning Knowledge, Activity Knowledge, Modeling Knowledge, and Teaching

Knowledge. These are also taught as kinsesthetic learning, visual learning, auditory learning and reading/writing learning.

Learning knowledge—I'm going to learn it. It is as simple as that. You learn about your desire. You actually do this more often than you think if you want to know more information on a subject and grab your phone to Google more information about it.

Activity knowledge is important to me because this is where most people fail. They will sit in the class, they'll learn all about it, and they'll get excited about it and feel pumped up and ready to go. But then when the time comes to go meet that person or go do a presentation, they'll make an excuse not to follow through. You've got to fail forward. You've got to go and do the activity. That's really where the knowledge is going to come in. But they're now Modeling Knowledge. That's what happened for me when I met my coach and my mentor. I began to model him.

HUMILITY IS
NOT A
PERSONALITY
TRAIT.
IT'S JUST
RECOGNIZING
THAT YOU
DON'T HAVE
SOMETHING.

Many people hear me on a conference call or speaking and they'll say, "You sound just like him," and they think that's an accident. No, it's on purpose. He has what I want. However, many people don't have that because of humility, the humility factor. Humility is not a personality trait. It's just recognizing that you don't have something.

When I first began my journey, I recognized that I didn't have the Bentley. I recognized that I didn't have the million-dollar home. I recognized I didn't have millions of dollars in the bank. The difference between me and someone else who wants those things is that I was humble enough to follow somebody who had what I wanted without envying them and guess what—two and a half years into my work, I have the Bentley. I have the million-dollar home. I've got my burning desire.

That's the deal. You must understand, to be humble and take the time to find a mentor and learn. Then you get into Teaching

Knowledge. Every person learns more when they teach. Most people who learn about this want to go from learned knowledge to teaching knowledge. They want to skip the activity knowledge and the modeling knowledge. You've got to go in the order of learned knowledge, activity knowledge, find somebody that you can model so that you can become worth modeling. Then you become the teacher and that's where the big money comes in.

Many of you have the learned knowledge and are willing to learn. You are reading this information so you can learn something. You join a conference call so you can learn something. You may go to a training or a seminar so you can learn something. However, it's important to note that people tend to hold back when it comes to the activity knowledge or they may start the activity but they don't continue the activity, There comes a point and time where it's absolutely required for them to really be able to set themselves up to be able to see results. If you are one of the many who start the activity but get distracted or get disappointed because maybe what you were doing just didn't seem to be working, then maybe it's time to revisit that vision.

CHAPTER 5

LIVE IN A VISION ENVIRONMENT

Part of the problem is fear. The fear of success. It's not even fear of failure. Well what if it works? As odd as it may seem, many people are afraid of that. And one of the things that I'm saying is you can only go where you can envision. It's like you've been driving and you're driving in the fog. You know where you want to go. You've probably already been there. You've seen other people get there but it's foggy. You can't see yourself. So what do you do? You've got to slow down. You can't accelerate because there's a fog around you. But once the fog clears away, now you can accelerate and move faster. That goes directly back to your vision. Many people believe in a vision board. Personally, I don't believe in a vision board, I believe in a vision environment. If you came into my place right now, you'd see pictures everywhere—everywhere! Why? Because I've got to remind myself of where I'm going. I cannot live in my present situation. I've got to continuously live in my future so every single day I'm working toward it. But what happens when you lose sight of where it is you're going and you start focusing on your present situation? Now all your thoughts are geared toward what's *not* happening as opposed to what's *going* to happen and you begin to internalize that. You become what you think about. *The Strangest Secret*, by Earl Nightingale is where I read "you become what you

I CANNOT LIVE
IN MY PRESENT
SITUATION.

I'VE GOT TO
CONTINUOUSLY
LIVE IN MY
FUTURE

SO EVERY
SINGLE DAY I'M
WORKING
TOWARD IT.

think about" – that floored me when I read that. I asked myself, "Is it really that simple?" Solomon, the richest man that ever lived, said, "As a man thinketh in his heart, so is he." I thought, "Wait a minute. Let me study where the thoughts come from. If I'm going to go down this path of continuously working, I'm led by my thoughts."

Where do thoughts come from? They come from my five senses. Every time I see something, it evokes a thought. I told myself, "Okay, what if I put things around me that I want to become my reality. Then I wouldn't stop, because now all my thoughts are geared toward what I want versus what is going on in my present life right now." So, it all goes back to that vision and that desire, what it is that you want out of your life.

My mentor lived about 30 minutes or so away from a very prosperous neighborhood. He used to drive to that neighborhood, especially on the weekends. The neighborhood had a gated entry to these multimil-lion-dollar estates and so on weekends they had open houses. My mentor would drive up there, give his driver's license and say, "Yes, I'd like to take a look at some of these open hous-es." He would go through that gate and would get a chance to see all of those mansions—all of those estates. Some of them would be open so you could stop by and take a look.

This is when he started to realize that ev-ery single one of these homes have libraries. Some of these homes—most of them—have movie theaters. He had never even thought about that! But now he thought, 'Wow, it's possible to have a movie theater in your home!' And it started giving him more things to put on his home vision process of what it is that he wanted to create for himself.

My mentor also used to go shopping in that area just to buy some grapes—anything so that he could have something that was also in that environment. That's how important it is to experience the environment in which you want to live. Simply going there and shopping for one small item is enough to give you the tangible nature of what it feels like to exist in that place where you wish to be.

CHAPTER 6

THE POWER OF BELIEF

You absolutely have to do what my mentor did. I believe that before you *get* there you must *go* there. And whatever it is that you experience in your life, you believe. Your belief system—the experiences you have had in your life up to this point—dictate to your senses what you believe is possible. Because you experience walking in that home, because you experience driving over there, even though it may seem as though it wasn't real, your belief system, your body, subconscious and senses, don't know what's real and what's not. You may say, "David, explain that to me."

If you've ever had a dream where someone was chasing you and you woke up right before they caught you, your body was sweating. Your heart was beating rapidly. You were still in the comfort of your own bedroom, but your body had no way of knowing if it was real or not. You *experienced* that dream. I would go to the Bentley dealership all the time and sit in the car. They would look at me like I was crazy because they saw what car I pulled up in and they would come and help me. I pulled up in a Malibu (the "Blue Boo Boo", that's what I called it). I would pull up the Blue Boo Boo and I would go sit in the car and just smell the leather. I would take pictures of it from the catalogues and put them up everywhere so that I had a chance to see it every single day. I had a chance to experience it. I did the same thing with homes. My mentor lives in that same subdivision where I bought my home. I would have to go there all the time and see his home and that made a huge difference. We're really talking about believing. That is going to be key to your success. You've got to experience the desire. You've got to experience what it feels like to be a multimillionaire before it happens, because if you don't experience it, you'll never believe it. Whatever you've experienced in your life, you'll believe. Right now, you're talking about conceiving it.

How do you conceive this vision of what it is that you're going to live into? From conceiving, you go to believing. How do you get yourself to believe it when it's not happening ... when it's not working for you? Then from believing, we want to take it to achieving. How do you actually achieve? Those are some of the steps that I want to cover in the information that we are sharing with people.

Once again, the conception part is just giving birth to an idea, giving birth to a vision—an environment. The whole key to that is your environment. Place yourself in the environment of that which you already see yourself as being in, so to speak. Do it through pictures but also do it through physically putting yourself around and surrounding yourself with the things that you actually have in some of these pictures, like going to the Bentley dealership and sitting in the car you want and so forth.

If you feel like you are just wasting the salesperson's time, then you are. You're not truly believing in your desire. You have to understand that you're just as deserving as anyone else. If you look at the words that are coming out of your mouth, you'll understand that life and death is in the power of the tongue. So, when you say, "I'm not going to be buying this Bentley," or, "I can't afford this Bentley," well, you just spoke that into existence. If something is happening in your life right now, whether it's lack, whether it's poverty, or whether your business is not moving, that means that particular situation is alive in your life. Life and death is in the power of your tongue, so that means that I can actually speak death into a certain situation. If I have no money, I can speak *death* to that. If I have a lot of money, I can continue to speak *life* into that. Does that make sense?

You can raise things up with your words. When you talk about going to the dealership and you're saying to yourself, "I don't know if I'll be able to purchase this," you just spoke that into your personal existence. Conceiving is when something goes inside of you. Your eye gate, your ear gate, these are all things going into your subconscious heart—which never sleeps and doesn't see things subjectively. It only understands what you tell it, and if you're telling it that you can't afford the car, your subconscious will create events in your conscious, waking world that continue to produce the belief that you can't have the the thing you desire. So watch your environment.

People often say that you're a product of

your environment. Think about the people that are around you ... who you let speak into your life. I don't let everybody talk to me—at all. Because now, whatever you're saying is going into my subconscious heart. And as a man thinketh in his heart, so is he. Therefore, I've got to be very careful who I let speak into my life, because that's going to be part of the whole that conceives me. I need somebody to tell me, "David, you're a multimillionaire." You need somebody to be telling you, "Yes, you can do it." You need those people around you. The people that don't believe in you need to be deleted from your life. Delete their name and their number from your phone. If you let them remain, you're carrying that baggage around with you and you have no idea, but they're actually pulling you down. Misery loves company, it loves it so much.

A lot of times, people get started in the industry of networking and they end up talking to their friends and family. Many times, their friends and family are the first people that are going to tell them that it won't work. Or ask, "Why are you doing that?" or say, "You're wasting your money," or, "You're going on another one of those training...." Someone might have a mom that's completely disempowering. Do they have to completely disallow their family? I believe that there should be a season of separation. I truly do believe that. I'm not suggesting to disown your family—nothing like that. But there has to be a season of separation.

What I would do, when I was living with my dad, when I would come home after prospecting all day or doing presentations all day was just go straight to my room and I would have personal self-development time. So even though I'd say, "Hey Dad, how are you doing?" and talk with him for a little bit, I'd go right up to my sanctuary which was that room with my twin size bed, and I had a little cassette player and that's where I was listening to all the tapes and all the books on audio to fill my mind. So even when I heard the negative things that I was going to hear anyway, like, "David, you need to go get a real job," (my dad used to tell me that all the time), and even though he believed in me, he was still saying I needed to go back to school, I would still keep the positive energy flowing into my mind. I didn't want anything to terminate that dream that I had … that goal that I had. What you've got to do is make your goal so big that yesterday dies. You've got to surround yourself with people that celebrate your goals; people that are encouraging you to accomplish your goals. If you don't have those people around you right now, if you get involved in this industry of network marketing, they're going to encourage you. Especially your upline. They've got a vested interest in making sure you are encouraged. Encouragement is why you always hear, "Read this book," "Listen to this audio," or, "Come to this convention or this particular seminar."

The Power of Belief

Many people think, "What are you talking about? I already went to a convention, why do I have to go to another one? I already read a book, why do I have to read another one? I already listened to an audio, you want me to listen to another one? Come on." It is important for people to constantly saturate their consciousness with this type of information.

Repetitious information is really the only way that you're going to be able to drive out doubt. Think about it, the information that you're listening to every single day is going to form the actions that you take. You MUST make it repetitious. It's paramount.

Years and years of listening to books and videos and audios and reading, those are things that you must do. If you don't have that, what's happening is you're listening to yourself and that was one of the mistakes that I was making. I was listening to myself ... but I had to finally realize the truth and have a discussion with myself.

CONCEIVE, BELIEVE, ACHIEVE

I had to be able to say, "Self, you're broke." I didn't want to get advice from a broke person, as opposed to listening to the Earl Nightingales and the Napoleon Hills. Those people who have what you want and can now give you the information that you need that can cause you to take the correct action that you need to take on a daily basis to be successful.

One of the things that I learned was raising the bar—raising your beliefs, which will in turn raise your actions, which in turn will raise your result. Believing really takes place when you are speaking the right words, when you have the right images, but more importantly when you have the right emotions. Those emotions have to be in check ... and those emotions are the emotions of faith, of excitement, and enthusiasm. Those things are very important to your success in this business.

So how does a person who is going through the motions as far as they're out there, they're talking to people, they've got this vision.

They are really excited about this vision.

They are starting to do some of the things that they've been instructed to do with regard to how the business works. But then a month goes by, six months goes by ... a year goes by, two years go by.

They look at their organization, they're making $100 a month, $200 a month, it just doesn't seem like things are happening.

They want it to happen as soon as possible because there are people that they see it is already happening for. They're impatient and that is working against them. Then they begin to wonder, "Maybe there is just something about me. Maybe that's why it's not working out for me." It's okay to want things to happen fast, but there are a series of events that need to take place and sometimes that is not instinaneous ... but that doesn't mean a person should just give up.

How can they strengthen their belief?

CHAPTER 7

YOUR BELIEF
SYSTEM

The first thing you've got to know is what impacts your belief. That's the very first thing. Then you have to believe in believing. Most people don't believe in belief. I think because of my background—both of my parents are pastors—much of the principles that we live by today are things that I learned when I was a little kid. Hearing that all things are possible to those that believe—all things, not just small things, made a huge difference. All things include whatever it is I can dream of,

IT'S SO
IMPORTANT
FOR YOU TO GO
TO THAT HOME
AND
EXPERIENCE
WHAT IT FELT
LIKE TO BE IN
THAT HOME YOU
WANT OR TO
SIT IN THE CAR
YOU'D LIKE TO
DRIVE.

EXPERIENCE IT
IN YOUR MIND.

whatever it is that I can think about, they are all possible if I believe. So let me learn what impacts my belief. Then I need to learn what grows my belief system. Lastly, I need to know how I really know that I am believing.

Most people don't know how to know they're believing. Most people don't know what the proof is, so to speak. What is the proof that you have? They say, "I believe" and I'm just looking at them like well you don't have the paid-off type of believing. So, when you talk about what impacts your beliefs, there are four specific things that impact your belief system. One is your environment, as previously mentioned. You've got to set your environment up for believing—you've got to do that. You have to set the environment up with pictures, with words, and different things around you that you will see all the time. I use index cards. I've got my own spe-cialty index cards—Louis Vuitton index cards. They have these words: "In the beginning was the Word." So every beginning, everything that I want to have, every genesis must start with a set of words. I write my words down and they're all around me, so everywhere I turn I have no choice but to see where it is that I'm going, what it is that I've written down. Words are spirit, but once I write them down, they become physical. I've taken something that is spiritual and put it in the physical. You've got to do that with your environment. Then, as also previously mentioned, you've got to have the right people around you. The giants that I've had a chance to work with, the people that I've had a chance to work with—I would have never met them if I wasn't around the right people. You must also listen to the right information. The information is going to be key to your belief system. Then there are the experiences that you give yourself. Most people only experience the past failures of their life, that's why they believe it so much. They believe that they've failed. They believe that nobody is joining the business because they have experienced failure and it is their belief. But what if you can take yourself out of that mindset and start experiencing the things that you want? That's why it's so important for you to go to that home and experience what it felt like to be in that home you want, or to sit in the car you'd like to drive. Then your belief system tells you, "Wow, it is possible for me to actually have that because I've experienced it."

What grows your belief are three things:
- The words that you're speaking,
- The images that you're looking at every single day
- The experiences, the emotions that you have.

You've got to have the right emotions. I'm going to delve into that because most people don't understand how to get themselves in the right emotional state at any point during the day. Something I learned from Tony Robbins is that you've got to be able to put yourself in the right state of mind. It's something that you're going to have to do with your body, your physiology, that's going to allow you to get in the right state right away that will cause you to take action. So, I'm speaking the right words, I'm seeing the right things, but now I've got to be congruent with my body to attain the right emotions that I need in order to take action. The paid-off type of believing, where you *know* that you're be-lieving can be identified by the following:

• P – you're patient. Most people don't have patience. You have got to be patient through this process.
• A – you've got to be constantly in activity mode. You've got to be constantly taking action.

You've got to stay inspired all the time, lis-ten to audios all the time, go to conventions all the time. But you've got to wrap it around with expectation. Don't go to an event or listen to an audio without expectation behind it. I expect that because I go to an event, inspiration is what's going to come out of it.

- D – is to be dedicated and disciplined. I've got to be dedicated to the cause; I've got to be disciplined. I believe that most people fail in this industry because they are lazy. Believing doesn't work if you're lazy.

Off just means paid off.

So, am I suggesting that if people show up lazy, there is just no luck for them and basically they're done? Is there any hope for somebody who is lazy? Well, if you're not willing to do the work that's necessary, I think you're being very disrespectful on your part to feel like you should have the same result as someone else who was willing to do the work. Everybody is going to have to pay a price. And whether you pay the price today, tomorrow or next year, you're going to have to pay the price. My belief system is that you can't make it in anything by being lazy. Now, do you have to work yourself to the bone? No. But you have to be persistent and consistent with any form of activity.

I teach people to expose two people per day. Anybody can do that. Anybody can expose two people per day. Well if you do that 30 days in a month, that's 60 new people you just talked to. You take that out 90 days or even 60 days and you've got 120 new people that you talked to, 180 people in 90 days. If we only went one out of 10, you've now sponsored 18 people in 90 days. Cut that amount in half and you've sponsored nine in 90 days. You can get some momentum sponsoring 9 people or 18 people in a 90 day span. If you're lazy, it all goes back to what do you really want. Is your desire strong enough? That's why you must expand your vision, expand your goals of what you want out of life. It causes you to take action. There are some things that you can do that will cause you not to be lazy anymore, but you've got to get up and go. You've got to go to that house and go to look at those cars. You'll be comfortable around people who are just like you. If I'm a hundredaire, (I don't know if that's real a word) and I'm hanging out with millionaires, I'm not comfortable. But if I stay in there, eventually I'm going to do whatever I have to do to be comfortable in that environment.

I'm going to have to make sure that I become a millionaire too, so that I can actually be in this environment. What most people do is say, "No, I don't want to go there because I'm not comfortable there, so I better leave there and stay right here." What you must remember is this: your comfort zone is your broke zone. If you're comfortable where you are right now—I don't care if you're a multimillionaire— if you are comfortable, that is your broke zone. You have to stay on top. You have to continuously dream bigger, continuously want more. So now your comfort zone has changed. Most people don't do that, but hopefully they will after reading this book.

Personally, I've have to continue to prove that believing works. I think we all have a responsibility to make sure that we prove that believing, hard work, and doing all the things that are necessary work. If I decide to stop and say, "Well, I've made it," then that means that somebody else that might be in my predicament, or maybe was in my predicament three years ago, four years ago, and they don't hear my story because I've stopped. They don't see that it's possible to move from one state in life to another and it's all relative. There are billionaires out there. They are looking at multimillionaires like, "What's wrong? You need to get on with it!" So, it's all relative and that's unlimited power that most people don't tap into. That's why I continue … because I know it's unlimited. But more importantly look at how many people are going to come along.

They will learn the information and implement it and they become multimillionaires.

So, I'm setting an example for other people or giving other people something to continue to strive and look up to just like my mentor. My mentor is continuously doing by moving forward and making an obscene amount of money—which obscenity is very good in that case. He's not stopping. He's still moving forward. Because I'm not comfortable ... I'm not comfortable around him because although what I have is good, there's another level I can attain.

However, if he stayed where he was when I met him, then all I could see is what I can see. But since he is continuously moving to other levels and he's helped so many other people, it keeps me uncomfortable and working to move up as well. When you look at people who I have mentored over the years, one specifically who is 28 years old and making an obscene amount of money as well, they are constantly growing and it's natural. There's nothing that is forced. You just love helping other people get to that next level. If I stay where I am, that means that you can't get to where I am. I must move off of that spot so that you can take that spot ... or even surpass me!

I told my mentor one time, "Listen, when I get to $30,000 per month I'm done. It's over. You're gonna have to pop my head, my head is going to be so big." Then when I reached that goal I had to ask myself, "What am I going to do with this?" You've got to keep moving forward. But that comes after achieving. That's a challenge for people that have already made it. If you listen to this audio right now and you're still in your process, it's imperative to understand that you've got to be patient. Not only do you have to be patient, you have to have peace. Think about it, you *become* what you think about. If I'm frustrated, guess what? My thoughts are born of frustration. I *am* frustration. Whatever it is I'm frustrated about, I'm bringing more of that into me. So, peace is essential. This is a peace that passes all understanding. I understand that my business is not moving fast enough but I still have peace. I understand that people are not showing up, but I still have peace. I understand that I'm not making millions of dollars or I'm not making $100,000 a year, but I still have peace. I still have the faith that is so important. I still believe in what I'm seriously working toward, because there is somebody that I have to become to be able to attract that amount of income. I'm not worried about the income, I'm now focused on who it is I need to become. Although this may seem counterintuitive if income is something you feel is imperative to your success, you have to understand that it's the peace, the state of mind, the focus, that will lead you to your desire. You will need to be the person who has the life you want regardless if you see it in your bank account or otherwise. Who you are is what will lead you to what you become.

Do I feel like I have become a different looking back at where I was just two and a half years ago compared to where I am now? I don't really think I became a different person. Two and a half years ago I was happy. Two and a half years ago I was excited. Four years ago I was happy, I was excited. If you met me four or five years ago you would have thought I was already a multimillionaire. I have always, for some reason, lived in my future. I never lived in my present. I always knew it was going to happen. So how would somebody else have believed that I was already a multimillionaire? In what ways? How I dressed? How I acted? How I talked?

Your self-image, your self portrait of who you are is important. Because how you see yourself is how other people are going to see you. Because I had been listening to *The Magic of Believing* and using the mirror technique and telling myself, "See, you believe you more than anybody else." I was telling myself that I was a multimillionaire. So when you met me, if I came to do a presentation at your home, I would not park in front of your home. I would park a couple of houses down. If we met at Starbucks, I would have parked way in the back.

I was always dressed appropriately. I was always dressed for success. No, I didn't have the custom clothing and all that good stuff, but guess what? I would buy it and then I would get it tailored to fit me. So, looking at me in custom made attire, I tell all my leaders, some of the folks who are not making money right now, to go and get custom made shirts. Go and get them. Because when you are sitting down with a person and they see your name on your cuff, automatically they think, "Oh, he's got to be successful because he's got his name on his cuff." I don't know if that's an actual truth for everyone, but I believed it was true. And it's not from the drycleaners, it was actual custom engraving. It may not be custom, just get them engraved, get your name engraved.

All of these things played a part because I saw myself but then also I had real people in front of me that had custom clothing. So we return to the concept of the environment again, because you've got to be around the right people. If I was around broke people, if I was around people that did not have what it was I wanted, then I would have exactly what it was that they had ... which is nothing. Whatever you're doing right now, you've got to stay connected to the leaders, you've got to be there at the weekly meetings, you've got to be at the events. You are constantly seeing what the end result looks like. It may be difficult for you to have that self-image right now because a lot of things may have happened in your life in the past that has caused you to not have the right self-image.

Remember, the things that caused you to have the wrong self-image were things that you were listening to, the things that you were seeing. You are going to have to change the things that you are listening to, you are going to have to change the things that you're seeing. You are going to have to change the people around you. That's why the season of separation is so powerful. Now I can hang around with family all day long because it's not going to bother me so much like it previously did because what they're saying now is, "I'm so proud of you." "I always knew you could do it." Not, "I knew you were going to do it. I always knew you were going to do it." "I was just playing with you before. Now can I get a loan?" And what do you do? You say yes, you can actually get some money. Because I don't loan money, you can actually have some money.

One of the things my mentor talked about in his program was about the "biggest belief that we believe." And the biggest belief that we believe are that lies are true, or that beliefs are true. Beliefs are nothing more than lies.

The only problem is that many people believe in things that are not empowering and are not going to move them toward where they want to go—and that's a lie. Believing that you can't do something is a lie. But also, believing that you can do it to some extent is a lie. So if you're going to have to tell a lie, you might as well tell a lie that's going to assist you in moving forward instead of a lie that's not going to allow you to move forward.

"There is nothing good or bad, only thinking makes it so,"—William Shakespear. There's no right or wrong, only your perception will cause you to believe what you think.

So, was I right to believe that I was going to become a multimillionaire? I believed it, and believing it made it so. You've got to give yourself that autosuggestion. You've got to tell yourself constantly over and over again what you believe about yoruself. Even if you don't believe it today because you cannot physically see it, keep telling yourself. That's why we talk about watching television. They are telling you a vision. You've now got to create that commercial that you're going to play over and over and over again *in your mind* of who it is that you're going to become. Everything that has happened to me was something that I told myself would happen and looped in my mind on replay. It's also best to do this in first person as opposed to seeing yourself in your mind in third person. I told myself it was going to happen and I had people around me that could assist me and help me to attain those goals.

Now some of you might say, "You know, I know of people who are producing the type of results I want to produce, but I'm so far away from those results that if I attempted to surround myself with them, what do I have to offer them? Do you think that they would say 'what are you doing here? Scat, scat, get away.'" This goes back to the self-image. They never looked at me like that because they only saw me how I saw myself. For the person who questions themselves, it has nothing to do with that other person telling you, "get away." It's really about you. Your self-image is not in line with being a winner because a winner can spot another winner. No matter where they are, it has nothing to do with money. You've got to put yourself in the situation where your leaders can actually see you performing.

Depending on what you're doing right now, you've got to put yourself in those leadership positions. Maybe you're doing the introduction. Maybe you're greeting people at the door. Whatever it is that you can do to let them know, "Hey, look, I'm here, I'm available," is wonderful. But it is equally important to have an assertive attitude about you. Wealthy people love that. They love people that serve—and that's going to be key to making sure that you're around the right people. And then it happens.

By using the law of attraction—you can actually write down, "I work with this person.

This person mentors me." And that which you belive to be true comes to pass. Recall how I met my mentor. It was through a series of events that took place. Then one day within this series of events, I found myself at his house. One thing my mentor explained to me was that if a person came to him while he was developing and generating a lot of wealth but they weren't really producing anything, he would evaluate their attitude. If they came to him with the proper attitude, then it didn't have anything to do with their money. To have a proper attitude, they needed to be willing to listen and implement the advice given to them, and he would be there for them. As of 2012, my mentor's in his 25th year of network marketing. He was so excited for them. He was amazed that they would go out and do something that he just shared— they actually *did it*. And then they would come back and he wanted to have them around. Attitude is everything. When you take those actions steps, your mentors will be really excited to work with you more and to talk with you more. So you've got to be willing to actually engage in some of the concepts to start taking some kind of action, too.

The systems that are in place allow you to be able to work with the top leaders in your company. Because they are on all the conference calls, and they are at all the trainings. But here's the deal … the same information that they are giving from stage or on that conference call is going to be the same information that they give to you on a one-on-one basis. You set the criteria in your mind that you need this one-on-one time. No, you don't; you need the information. If you take the information and go apply it and demonstrate the success, they'll be calling you. They'll look at their organization and say, "Okay, this must be somebody that's taking the information that I'm giving on these conference calls and these trainings that I'm doing and now they're implementing it. Now I can take them in and help them understand and grow from where they currently are."

There has to be a respect of the mentor's time as well. If you have to mentor 30,000 people right now, it would be impossible. You can only mentor a few people and those will be the ones who have taken the information you've given them and are moving forward with it—really implementing it. That's the decision that everybody must make ... the decision of, "I'm going to take this information, implement it and have success." Then a mentor will be able to say, "Yes, you're worth me coaching, you're worth my time."

In the end, your imagination and your vision are your choices, therefore, how you choose to move forward with your belief and action is also your choice.

Once you decide to use these tools that every one of us naturally possesses within us, along with the desire to be mentored because you understand the value it will bring, then whoever you choose as your mentor will believe in you as well. The choice of your belief will make or break your success.

CHAPTER 8

WE BECOME WHAT WE THINK ABOUT

I have mentioned a number of books that had a large impact on my success. For example, *The Magic of Believing* by Claude Bristol, *Think and Grow Rich* by Napoleon Hill, and *The Strangest Secret* by Earl Nightingale. I made references to Tony Robbins' *Unlimited Power*. Another book mentioned is *Building a Network Marketing Business* by Jim Rohn. I must have listened to that for a year. My mentor is actually the person who recorded that audio! If you put that audio on right now, I could actually speak it verbatim.

For a year straight, that was huge for me. Also, *Think and Grow Rich* had a huge impact on me. Two audios that really inspired the shift in me were *The Magic of Believing* by Claude Bristol and *The Strangest Secret* by Earl Nightingale. Those are the two that most definitely changed my perspective. I remember sitting down at a leadership event that we were having and I had only been involved for about four months. We had about 50 people attending and it was a private leadership event that we were presenting. I asked my mentor, "You have the nice car, you have the nice home, you're successful. Why is it that nobody else is like you?" I was asking facetiously. His response is what has completely led me down this path to where I am today. He said, "Nobody believes the way I do."

I said to myself, "That's it? You're telling me

I'VE BECOME
THE PERSON
I AM TODAY
BASED ON MY
THOUGHTS.

IF I WANT TO
CHANGE
SOMETHING IN
MY LIFE
WHATEVER IT IS

ALL I HAVE TO
DO IS CHANGE
MY THOUGHTS.

it's this whole believing thing? Okay. So then I began to study it so anything that had anything to do with believing, I made sure I was listening to it. When I read *The Magic of Believing* and he explained the mirror technique and delved into the power of suggestion, I began to implement all of that information. I never met Claude Bristol, he passed away. People who think, "Oh, I need to be mentored by somebody," ... mentorship is important, but the information that you can listen to can allow you to now attract that mentor. *The Strangest Secret* – we become what we think about. I became what I thought about.

It's extremely important to keep your thoughts focused on the positive. I don't mean you must be a happy Pollyanna type all of the time, but I do mean that you cannot clutter your mind with thoughts of what the worst outcome could be or what type of worst case scenario will ruin you. "For the thing which I greatly feared is come upon me, and that which

WE BECOME WHAT WE THINK ABOUT

I was afraid of is come unto me." - Job 3:25 We cannot let the thoughts that contain our fear dictate the outcome of our life. Man's greatest adversary is fear. "Fear is a thought in your mind, and you are afraid of your own thoughts" - Joseph Murphy. Your thoughts must be tamed and you can train yourself to think only of that which you desire, and in doing so you will dictate the outcome of your future situations.

I've become the person I am today based on my thoughts. If I want to change something in my life, whatever it is, all I have to do is change my thoughts. Well where do my thoughts come from? We examined it earlier. They come from the five senses, and I also believe thoughts come from God and also from the enemy. I can control my five senses. When I taste something, that sense invokes a thought—the feeling of taste and how it resonates with your mind and body. Tastes can even bring memories, which are thoughts. When you smell something, touch something, you're thinking naturally of that feeling of doing so.

I was listening to *25 Secrets of Wealth Creation* by Kevin Trudeau and in the very beginning he talked about *The Magic of Believing*. He talked about *The Strangest Secret*. I listened to that back in 2006. But now, years later, after being in the right environment and actually being around somebody that was listening to it or already heard it and having them suggest to me to listen to it, too. I went back and listened to it again after all that time. But when I went back and listened to *25 Secrets of Wealth Creation* it made me realize that this man told me what I should be listening to back in 2006. I didn't have to wait until 2009 or 2010 to get this information if only I had been paying attention. I wasn't paying attention. You can listen all day long but not actually pay attention.

In *25 Secrets of Wealth Creation*, he gave me the secret right then at the very beginning, *The*

Strangest Secret, but I didn't go seek out the information. See that's the thing for you right now, talking about all these books. I listened to *The Magic of Believing* for at least five months straight. I didn't listen to any other audio for five months. If I was on the phone with someone doing a three way call, it was playing in my other ear. I had the phone to one ear and I had *The Magic of Believing* playing in my other ear.

I kept it playing just in case something negative was said to me that would try and plant a seed of doubt ... just in case a person said something like, "That's a scam or a pyramid scheme." *The Magic of Believing* would negate anything of that nature. You've got to loop it over and over in your mind so that it sinks in beyond just your conscious level of thinking. As I mentioned, if you played the audio of *The Magic of Believing* right now, I could speak it verbatim. If you played *The Strangest Secret* right now, I could say each word verbatim. You've got to plant those ideas in your deeper mind, where your belief systems exist. In 2008 I even played *Think and Win Big* while I was sleeping! That was with my mentor, Johnny Wimbey and Les Brown. That's the thing, when you find that information, when you find that audio that really speaks to you, you have got to stay on it. You have got to stay on it because it you've got to meditate day and night, day and night, day and night. So when you find that audio that speaks to you in such a way, you must do that. Have I listened to all those audios? No, I haven't. But once I found one that really spoke to me—one that I believed in and with which the information resonated, then I stayed on it to master it.

Now it's gotten to the point where the person that actually gave that audio, read that book or even wrote the book ... I probably know the information just as well or more thoroughly than them—because remember, they're not listening to it every single day, looping it over and over. I've got a training out that somebody recorded; it's on You-Tube, "The Win Formula". It's based on the idea of rob and duplicate ... rob and duplicate all the way to multimillionaire status. Of course, you have to put your own twist in there. That's the key because we don't want to get anyone in trouble here thinking they can just go take any of my mentor's programs—or anyone's programs, and duplicate them. These are programs that you buy. Use the information. Don't sell the information—use the information, that's key.

CHAPTER 9

HOW TO BUILD A NETWORK MARKETING ORGANIZATION

Of course, these tips will be from a generic standpoint, but what are some keys, what are some processes? What are the ways that you can go from conceiving, believing to achieving? It's interesting because one of the things we were talking about earlier is the importance of having a skill set.

You've got the desire plus the skillset and

you add the faith. They're all really important ingredients and the way to get the skillset is by action. You have to learn what to do, but then you have to utilize that activity knowledge. So if someone is just getting started in the industry, they are just getting started in this business of networking, or whether they've been around for a while, it doesn't matter. There are still key steps that are really important for people to do to become successful in this business and there are always things that you can pick up and learn. Our world is always changing.

The very first thing I would recommend a person to understand is that this is a business. It is not network marketing, it's not multi-level marketing, it is a real business and you've got to treat it as such. When you look at it, as any traditional business, you are going to need capital. You are going to need some funds. You need something to actually put into the business that is going to allow it to really accelerate. In this type of business, it's not money that is needed. It is really people. So people are your capital. People are the things that you're going to need, the resources that you are going to need that are going to allow you to be successful in this business. One of the first things that we teach people just getting started obviously is begin building a list. That's if you're dealing with your warm market.

There are three different phases that you're going to be dealing with. You're going to have your warm market, you're going to have your hot market and then you're going to have your cold market. Your millions of dollars that you are going to earn are typically going to come from your cold market, the people that you don't even know right now. Understand that your warm market is going to be practice. You can become well versed in performance in this business so that when you meet somebody who you don't know, you've already practiced enough on mom and dad and friends and family that know exactly what to say to this person. So really categorize that list. One of the things that I tell people, whether you are out prospecting the cold market or whether you are writing your initial warm market list, is that you are putting your capital together. You want to have the five points first.

First, here is some clarification about the markets. Your warm market consists of people that you know. Your hot market consists of people you know that know someone and will introduce you. Now they are introducing you to somebody that they know. That is your hot market because now a three-way synergy is really taking place now. That person is going to trust you and respect you because that person is introducing you to them. Your cold market is someone you *don't* know. These are people you might meet at the market or at Starbucks. Those are the three markets that you will be going after. Within that, really what you're looking for are the following five characteristics:

- People that are 25 and older
- People that are married
- People who have children
- People who own a home
- People who make an income of $40,000
- $80,000 per anum

When I look back on all the people in this industry of network marketing that have major success, they all somewhat fit that demographic of those five pointers. Another way that you want to categorize your list is the four checkers:

- People that have a center of influence
- People that are self-starters
- People that have the means to get started in the business

The fourth characteristic is to find people who can be taught and have a coachable spirit, that have the humble spirit to want to learn about the business. Those are the things that you're looking for.

Because if you can understand the basics of this business, it's very simple. You talk to a lot of people, you make a lot of money. You talk to a little amount of people, you make little money. I think that if people understand that it's a numbers game. That's all this business is about. But understanding the things that we talked about in this book first, believing and speaking it and seeing it—will allow you to continuously take the action steps that allow you to be successful in this business. Then you've got to make sure that whatever opportunity that you're in right now has a system in place.

System stands for: Saving Yourself Time Energy and Money. There has to be a road map in place for a brand new distributor that is getting started, that knows that these are the steps that must be followed. Thus, we have a four step system where everybody knows this is what they must do to be successful in this type of business. Therefore, you've got to make sure that whatever business you're in, you've put together a road map for a brand new person to actually get involved and now you can enter into how to go about building the business.

CHAPTER 10

THE PS3

Prospecting – I call this the PS3 – piquing interest, showing the plan and then doing a three way call. Piquing a person's interest that is on your list is very important. Let us say you are meeting somebody to chat. Now your goal is to show them the plan. There are various different ways in which you can show the plan. It may be an online presentation, it may be a conference call, it may be a PBR or something like that, or maybe a weekly meeting.

There are so many different ways that you can expose opportunity to people. You must do that three-way call, it is the validation step. You get them on the phone with a person that can validate the information directly. It doesn't really take a lot of money, it's going to take *some* money, but it doesn't take a lot of money. The main capital in this business is people. And on the list there are some different check points and different characteristics.

Now for example, what if a person isn't married?. Do you just not check that? Do you take them off of your list? Take whatever points that they have and if the person has three out of five, I'll put the three by their name. If they have a four out of five I'll put a four by their name. Now I know this is a person that I need to call right away. So that's my power 30 list. I want to initially call 30 people right away that fit anywhere from four to five of those checkers, of those pointers. Now I'm talking to the right people right away. Most people fail in this industry because they don't talk to enough people and they don't talk to enough of the right people.

There's no way for you to actually know who the right person is because that's pre-judging and if you think you know but you're saying that you can get a pretty good clue of the demographics by checking out some of these pointers. Now what if they are a two or three? Do you just never call them, or do you call them on your down time when you don't have anything else? You *do* call them, but that person now has to have major desire. For me to keep calling them and going over and over … that person has to have the desire that they want to win. Because desire, hunger, those are the only attributes that can take care of a person that doesn't have those pointers. Like myself. When I got involved in this industry I had none of those pointers. But I had desire, I had the hunger. So I was a perfect prospect that people were looking for because I was hungry, literally and figuratively. But most people are not going to be like me, getting involved in this industry at a young age and earning millions of dollars. Most people are not going to do that. It's going to be the 25 and older, the married, the kids own a home and all that good stuff. That's really who is going to go out and build this thing. Because now they have reasons. You are really looking for people that have a reason.

In the very beginning of your business, you've got to now develop the WHY. That's the very first thing you want to do is develop the why. Why am I doing this business? Why am I involved in this type of business right now? What am I looking to get out of this business? So it all goes back to setting some goals. One of the most important things I learned from Zig Ziglar about setting goals—there are six steps to actually accomplishing them. One is you have to have a goal. Have it written down. Number two is you have to

PEOPLE ARE
GOING TO
REJECT YOU.

THEY ARE GOING
TO LIE.
DECEPTION IS
GOING TO COME
IN.

YOU ARE
GOING TO HAVE
TO OVERCOME
THOSE FOUR
MENTAL
ENEMIES.

have a date of completion. You must set a date of of completion for what it is you are looking to accomplish. Then you have to list the obstacles. They are going to try to stop you from accomplishing your goals. Most people don't do that. Those obstacles are those four mental enemies. Those four mental enemies, they're going to come. If you haven't experienced them already, 1 promise you, they're going to come. People are going to reject you. They are going to lie, deception is going to come in. Attrition is going to come, and apathy is going to come in. The first two mental enemies have to do with people joining your business. The last two have to do with when people do join your business, what happens with them after the fact. Attrition – people are going to quit. Apathy – people are going to lose their dreams, lose their goals. So you've got to understand that you are going to have to overcome those four mental enemies, those obstacles. And obstacles are really what is going on inside of you – the enemy (ene ME). Whatever is going on inside of you is what is going to cause you to not continuously move on. So once you've identified the obstacles, now you want to identify the people you're going to be working with. Who am I going to be working with who's going to help me help them be successful? See, most times when we get involved in this business our first goal is to make all the money. Our first goal is for us to become successful. But if you take it off of *you* and then put in all the *people*, who can I help be successful?

Put together that plan, that plan of action. How many people am I going to talk to on a daily basis. You've got to set a goal. One of the things that I learned is the 10 core commitments. I learned that from Jeff Olson. The 10 core commitments. I've got to make sure that I'm executing a game plan interview. I'm going to find out what you want out of the business, because if I'm bringing you into it and investing my time and energy, I want to know why you're doing it. Then I can remind you when you're ready to quit about some of the things you told me in the beginning—didn't you tell me you're doing this for your mom? Didn't you tell me you're doing this for your daughter? So now I've got some ammunition to make sure that you stay in the game. And then also, we teach people to expose two people per day. Just doing that small activity on a regular basis is going to allow you to be successful in this business. Therefore there are 10 of them that we'll examine throughout this book regarding how to really build growth. Once I've identified the people I'm working with, I'll put that plan of action in place. The sixth step is now making sure I have something in it for me. What's in it for me? That is going to be key and a lot of companies have incentives out there for you to go out there and build the business, so you know if you do this, if you hit this rank you get this. And most people don't build the business for money. They build the business for recognition.

The PS3 is what you're going to do with your list. You're going to pique their interest. And how you pique their interest is you've got to develop a power phrase. Then you're going to show the plan. Then the three way call. It's a video game – pique, show, call. Some of the power phrases that we've utilized, knowing what you know now about whatever particular industry that you're in. If you had the ability to go back 10 years and invest, would you have done it? Another phrase that you can use is – Right now today do you keep your income options open? If I told you I found a way for you to make a fortune on the internet, using only 5 – 10 hours of your time a week, is that something that would be interesting to you? But a lot of power phrases that I use have to do with my business. So one of the phrases that I've used that has worked tremendously is—knowing what you know now about Starbucks, if you had the ability to invest in Starbucks 10 years ago, would you have done it? Or Facebook, or Microsoft? It depends on how old the person is. You would have done it all day. Well listen, I found something bigger than Microsoft. So that's the whole thing about piquing though, is you're peaking their interest to really see if whatever you say is something that this person may actually be a prospect or not. If they're not piqued than maybe they are a suspect and not a prospect.

Now if they are a suspect, in other words if they don't get piqued, do you give them another pique in interest phrase, or do you just kind of let them go? Do you chase someone around to pique them? The answer is that If you have a strong list, then you're not going to chase anybody. So that posture is going to be important where you've got a list of 200 – 300 people that you have written down. So if I tell you that and that doesn't get your juices flowing, automatically you are letting me know that you are not the person I'm looking for. Remember I'm looking for four aces. So I need to go through this deck of cards as quickly as possible right now so I can get to the four aces. If I say something like that to you that I know really got me going and it's gotten thousands of other people going and it didn't get you going, then more than likely you're not the person that I'm looking for. I'm going to move on to the next person. I may put you on a 30 day follow up list. I like to say the fortune is in the follow up.

What is different for me now is that you make a fortune and then you follow up. So if I talk to you about it today, and you say, "Well no, I'm not really interested," I'll go away and make a fortune and I'll follow up with you later on. I think by then you'll be ready. Firstly, people are not running around begging and chasing people. Number two, if someone is really just not open, they are just not open right now but they could be open later on, but don't sit there and wait for them to be open. And then number three – one of the keys that you're talking about that is really important with regard to piquing a person's interest and so forth is that if a person is ready then great, they're ready. So, what if they are ready? In other words, what if they say, "Sure, I keep my options open." Here's what you should do next.

You want to show them the plan. With all systems that are in place right now, you want to have something that is quick and easy so that you can actually get information in front of them right away. It is imperative to do this because you may not be able to get in front of everybody. This person may live in another city or even another country. There could be an online presentation that's available. Perhaps there's an on demand opportunity call that's available.

Because of the different ways in which people get in contact with one another and the vast array of locations where people are from, I created a call where as soon as you dial into it, it begins. For example, I would call you and say, "Hey listen, knowing what you know now about Microsoft, if you had the ability to invest in Microsoft 10 years ago, would you have done it? Yes? Well, there's a call that's going to be taking place in the next 10 minutes, I need you to listen to it." When I make these types of calls, understand that with that you've got to make sure you're operating with the four Es.

Let me give you a clear idea of what I call the **four Es** – you're **excited**, you're **enthusiastic** about what it is you're calling about, you already understand that you're going to **expose** hundreds of people so you're not really attached to that person saying yes or no. Lastly, you have great **expectation** that the person hearing you is going to receive the information.

Because of this, I'm in a hurry when I'm on the phone and I'm definitely going to demonstrate the value to the listener.

I pique the interest of the listener, who is my prospect. I might say, "Hey listen, my mentor, I don't really have much time to talk, but something just came across my desk. Knowing what you know now about Microsoft (Starbucks, Facebook or any other large, profitable company), if you had the ability to invest 10 years ago would you have done it? Absolutely. Listen, I found something bigger than Microsoft. There's a private call that's going to be taking place in the next 15 minutes. Can you carve out 20 minutes of your time to listen in and tell me what you thought about what you heard on the call?"

There are some key things that I make sure I say. The call is 20 minutes. What does that make it? It makes it quick and easy. I make sure to say it's a private call. I make sure to say that I don't have a whole lot of time, but I thought of that person because I knew that they understood business. I want them to listen to it because I have a lot of other people I need to call.

This demonstrates value and then takes it away. I don't have time to answer all the questions. I'm brand new, I might not know all of the answers. Therefore I want to make sure that the system does the work for me. Even if you do know all the answers, you still want the system to do the work for you, because now this person is thinking, "If he's giving all the answers, do I have to be as good as him? Well I don't want to be that good. I don't want to do that." They might even go back to that believing factor then and think, "I don't believe I can do that."

I'll end the call by saying, "Listen, I've got to go, I've got a lot of other people to call; what I'll do is follow up with you later. I'll let you know that it's worked and I'll get back to you."

You absolutely must to do that with certain people. You must do it in a very respectful way, but you have to let them know that *your time is valuable*, but you'll go make it and then come back and get the person.

So now you've given them some informa-tion—regardless of whatever the type of sys-tem that you're using through your line of sponsorship. In your case, you have a 20-min-ute sizzle call, which is actually a form of presentation. The listener is given a pre-sentation on that particular call. So what happens after that? Do you teach to fol-low up within a particular period of time?

What I typically do is I tell that person to call me back. What I'm really doing is testing them. I'm evaluating if this person is truly ready. If they call me back, that means that I've got someone interested. If I call them back, and ask them if they had a chance to listen to the call and they say yes—great. I follow up with questions like, "What did you like best about what you heard on the call?" They'll respond with what they liked and then I'll say, "Well listen, I'm working with some of the top indi-viduals. The top individual can be somebody who's only been in business for two weeks.

The PS3

They are leading a national expansion team right now, and I'm working with them. And they told me that if I talk to somebody and they got a chance to listen to that call and they love what they heard, definitely get them connected on the phone. My goal now is to get them on the phone with the expert. Now I'm going to edify the expert. Edification is going to be key when you are actually building this business. Learn how to speak well of other people. I'm going to edify my expert to this prospect... "Well (my prospect), I'm going to get you on the phone with this young lady. She's an incredible young lady. She actually used to be a school teacher and five months into this particular business she's been able to walk away from her full-time job. Now she's a multiple six figure earner with this opportunity. I want to see if I can get her on the line with you. She's extremely busy but she told me that if I found somebody that was like you, she'd take a moment out to talk with you for a second."

After five months, this particularly successful lady walked away from a career that wasn't fully meeting her needs. The multiple six figures came later; however, she got the ball rolling which is a good point to make. I got her on a three-way call with my interested person, or prospect. What's the purpose of the three-way call? How do you teach people? Many people are listening and they're saying, "Okay, three-way calls, yeah, I've heard about three-way calls." Some people may have not fully utilized the power of three-way calls. Some because they may not understand to make a three-way call, and others because they don't feel comfortable doing it. Whatever the case may be, they must understand the purpose of the three-way call and its potential.

There are many different purposes to a three-way call. One of them is to validate the information that the person has actually just heard. Another reason is for that expert to actually edify you back to the prospect. The prospect is going to be working with you and the prospect wants to know that you have the capabilities to help them be successful in the business. Furthermore, that expert is actually going to move them along. We have a specific word—bamfaming—which means book a meeting from a meeting. That person may be ready to get started off from that one conference call. They may be ready to get started after an online presentation. But guess what? They may not be ready. Now that expert says hey listen, David is having a coffee and jazz mixer at his place on Tuesday at 7:00. Can you make it out there so you can actually get a live picture of what's taking place right now with this project?" Now, the expert is doing the inviting. Considering the way people are in general, very rarely will someone stand up a stranger versus standing up somebody they know.

At this point, this is where you mention the word private business reception, for the people who have never heard that terminology, it's simply a home meeting. To change the perception of the home meeting, call it a coffee and jazz mixer or a juice party. Someone else may call it a tea party. Whatever names people are using for whatever they are doing are all indirect ways to refer to a home meeting.

Let us say that people are at a private business reception. What happens there? What is the purpose of a private business reception as far as what is happening?

Are they doing a presentation? Will it be live? Yes, there will be a live presentation that will take place. However, the reality is that it is giving them a chance to come out and experience the product or the service, whatever it may be, so that they can actually see it firsthand. Remember whatever it is that I experience, *I will believe.* There are going to be other people there, and most people are followers. They see other people getting started and they're going to get started, too. Therefore, what you need to do at those meetings is keep them very informal. Don't change anything up in your house, keep it very normal. Keep it professional but make sure people understand what it is they're coming to see. You may have a video that you play that truly demonstrates it. But the confidence that you have when you actually give them the application and say, "Let's get you enrolled in what it is we're doing. I started at one of the highest levels and I believe that you should get started there, too." In taking those steps repetitiously, and by teaching people to do it at least four times a week, we build the habit of confidence and repetition.

PS3 essentially goes back to the concept of piquing interest—show the plan. In the middle of showing the plan, I'm specifically talking about the private business reception, which is the home meeting. It's very important for people to understand that the home meeting is going to be the basis of your business. What you want to do is start developing interest during these meetings.

Here's the key thing: you've got to develop one to two people per month that are going to be committed to actually showing the plan four times a week. That is key. If you're the only one showing the plan in your organization, then you're the only one that has a business. But when you start developing one to two people per month and you teach those people to do the same exact thing, you can see your business grow tremendously. The key is to keep it very simple—nothing complicated. If something is complicated, then people do not want to do it. But if I keep it very concise with simple systems, then I am able to demonstrate it with simplicity. If it's a video that I play, then maybe it's a YouTube presentation that I created to demonstrate all of my talking points and keep everyone engaged with the information.

The PS3

I began doing this with a PowerPoint on DVD. I would actually just put it in the DVD player and turn it on. I used a PowerPoint DVD and then I had so many people showing the plan over and over again and we were just developing one or two people per month doing it the same thing over and over again. Now there are more options. You can record yourself with the technology we all carry in our hands and create a video that can be shared easily through email or even on platforms like YouTube or private Facebook groups. As times change, our method of delivery of information changes.

I'm teaching these points to my organization—to develop one or two people a month who are basically doing this type of business reception. They're actually piquing interest, getting people on the calls and so forth. They will work on a three-way call and get people to private business receptions. At a private business reception, showing the plan lasts

CONCEIVE, BELIEVE, ACHIEVE

from 30 to 40 minutes. It's not a marathon by any means. The mixer/get-together part can be fun. You've got light music playing, all that can take some time. But the actual presentation of the business really should be 30 – 45 minutes max. You will lose people's interest after too long. Studies have shown that between 20-30 minutes is the average time a person will give attention to a presentation, and if it's not catchy enough, that time diminishes. We are now in the era of even shorter attention spans with smartphones and constant access to content, so you are even more likely to lose the attention of people if they think they can stop for a moment and check their social media feed or a news alert. In fact, there's a reason Instagram videos are short and then have an option for you to click and watch more. The key is to hook you, and then to entice you to want to watch the full video.

The imperative point for you as a brand-new distributor is to know how to develop that vision. If you don't have the vision right now, whatever opportunity that you're involved in should have a vision that you can buy into. You are going to share the vision of the company. You are going to share the vision of what it is that you see. Then you are going to invite them to be a part of your vision.

"Hey, we're going to capture 5% of this particular market. Right now, we've already captured 1%. We're going to capture 5%. This is what is going to happen over the next three years. Do you want to be a part of what it is we are doing? I'm a part of it and I'm excited. This is what is already happening. I'm going to give you an application to get yourself started. There are different levels you can start at. This is the level I started at." Always let people know where you began. Whether it's one of the lowest levels or not, let them know that you're in the game, then give them the application.

Your belief and you doing it over and over again and developing the skill is what will make you great. Will you be great at this the first time? No, honestly. I remember I stood up one time to do a presentation and my mind sat back down. You're going to do it over and over and over again. And guess what? It will actually become part of your subconscious. That's where the skill part goes into play. In the beginning you must do it consciously. I must be conscious when I'm doing a three-way call. I must be conscious when I'm doing a presentation. This is similar to when a person first learns how to drive.

As a new driver, you were very conscious of what you were doing. You were very focused. No texting, no talking—nothing. Then, by driving over and over again, things seep into your subconscious. It has been proved to be a form of hypnosis, actually. You don't need to tell yourself "green means go". You know sub-consciously that green means go, so you do. So by doing the presentation over and over again, it allows you to go into your subconscious where you don't have to think about it while you drive. You don't have to think about it while you're doing a presentation.

It's kind of like what Malcolm Gladwell talks about in his book called *Outliers*. One chapter details that in order for you to master anything, it's going take you practicing 10,000 hours. Whether or not it's 10,000 hours as the exact amount ... who knows. But if you take a look at my first four or five years, four and a half years or so, maybe I did put in 10,000 hours during that time. It felt like it!

Whatever it is, it just means practice—a *lot* of practice. I did put in a lot of repetition, over and over and over again, even when it wasn't working. I kept doing it over and over again and when I started getting bored a little bit, I kept doing it. *Repetition is everything*, even when reading these words. Points I make are repeated for a reason. When I was thinking, "Oh man, is this ever going to happen?" I kept repeating and eventually this is when this whole compounded effect, this magic kicks in so to speak and something great happens. Now with the private business reception, is there one person doing the presentation, are there two people doing the presentation? Does it really matter? Is it just a matter of the system that the person who is listening may have with their organization?

If you are the host, you may be hosting the event and your sponsor might come over to do the presentation—that would be ideal. But if you see that your sponsor can't be there, you'll want to use the system. Maybe a recording on your laptop that you can connect to a TV, perhaps an online presentation for you to show the plan to them—whatever you're more comfortable with is what you should use. You don't want to use technology you're uncomfortable with and flop yoru presentation. The bottom line is that you've got to understand that people are going to get involved. That's the mindset that you've got to have. *They are going to get involved.* Whatever way you show the plan to them, if they came to the event, they came for a reason. But remember, what I always recommend for people to do, even before a person comes out to a presentation—whether it's the weekly meeting or whether it's a private business reception—I recommend to make sure that the person has seen or heard the presentation before they came. That's where that 20 minute call that you have already had will come in. That's the qualifier. Think about it ... you get a chance to listen to that call and you like it, and I tell you I'm having a coffee and jazz mixer. You come after you listen to that call and you are coming to get involved.

When a person makes the decision to get started, they say, "Okay, I'm in, I'm ready to get going." So now what do you do next when the person is brand new and they are just getting started? They ordered whatever their pack is and they say they want to build a business so it's a business building perspective, where do you go from there? There are three laws of building and this right here has made all the difference in my business. Getting people involved in any business is very simple. You talk to a lot of people. Go back to the basics of talking to people. It's a numbers game. You've got to understand the three laws of building: Number one—a recruit, someone who joins your business is not a recruit until *they've* gotten a recruit. In certain businesses, it's not until they've created their dual team. Until they've gotten their duel team … until they've actually sponsored somebody in this business, they're not in the business. You, as the business builder, as the person that's looking to get to the next level, have to know that when I sponsor John into the business, John is not in the business yet until I help him get his dual team.

Until you help John sponsor someone—until you help John really go through the process that's required to make those calls that you're talking about in order to put someone else through the process, in order to expose a person to the point where the person says, "Yes, I'm in now," then you really can't say you have a recruit or a new person in your business. Many people just get someone signed up and they think, "I've got them, I've got them!" In reality, you don't really have anything.

The first law of business then is that a recruit is not a recruit until *they* have a recruit. What happens is if you sponsor someone and you celebrate and you forget to get in that person's warm market right away, then you've got to get back to the cold market. But if you can now get in that person's warm market, you can just stay warm. I'd rather be warm than be cold. Referrals that you don't know might not trust you. But if you are working with someone that they know, they trust that person. Then you've got a trust factor which has opened up, but maybe the person they know they don't really respect when it comes to business cause they don't know them as a business person. But YOU are the business person so you got the respect and the trust and that's one of the main things that's important. The triangle effect is really important.

The second law, after you have the first law down, the second law is that a recruit leg of business is not a leg until you have driven it four levels deep. For example, I sponsor John. John is not a recruit until he has a recruit. That recruit is now on my second level. Now you've got to implement the first law with that second recruit to get it down to my third level.

The same thing must happen with the third, get it down to the fourth level. Once I've taken that leg four levels deep, now I've got a leg of business. Here's the caveat to that. Whenever you take a leg four levels deep—every time you do this—you're going to find a superstar. I can go leg after leg after leg of people that I've gone four levels deep in and every

single time, I was able to identify a superstar that could do what it is that I'm doing.
Now the third law—this is where people miss
it. They think, "Man, I've got three people on
my team, I've got a team. My team this and
my team that." No, you don't have a team
until you've driven that leg eight levels deep.
Eight levels deep. And now you work with
that person. What I'll do is take that person
that is the fourth level from me, treat them
like they are my first level and take them another four levels deep. Remember, you are
building a tree—a tree that is deeply root-
ed is one that is going to stand the test of
time. Never forget this. Anytime that you
take a leg eight levels deep, it will produce
business for you for the rest of your life.

Every PBR that I'm doing, it's all within the
back of my mind that I'm going deep in this
leg. I'm going wide, you want to personally
enroll a lot of people and that's really going to
be the wealth. But the security in your busi-

ness is going to be the depth. So when I'm in your home, what I'm thinking is, "Who do you know?" When I sponsor you, who do you know? I'm in that person's home. As a leader I'm going four levels deep. When I find that superstar, I'm going to go another four levels deep and that becomes eight levels deep. Now I've got two leaders because now I've got two superstars in that one leg that I can coach, train, build and help them do what it is that I'm doing. To help those one or two people per month showing the plan four times a week. This is how exponential growth takes place.

When my mentor sat down with me and he showed me this, he showed me the calendar training. He said, "David, if you do this for 18 months, money will never be an issue for you ever again. It takes 18 months, it takes a series of 90 day blitzes for you to become successful in this business." A series of 90 day blitzes. You get the first 90 day blitz to really get yourself skilled in what it is that we're doing. I think it takes a person 90 days of being involved in the business, of showing the plan consistently, to develop the skill of somebody that can actually produce a large amount of volume. 90 days. If you can be committed for the first 90 days to simply learn how to do an effective presentation, the next 90 days will show you how to help other people do the same exact thing. So now you're six months into the business. At six months into the business, not only are you well integrated in how to do a presentation, but now you've taught three to five other people. And with three to five leaders in your organization, the next six months, the next year.

I look back at where I was at the beginning of 2010. I had been involved in the business for not quite a year because I began on April 22nd, 2009. In the beginning of 2010, I was already earning a multiple five figure a month income. I was working with a school teacher, with a postal worker and a federal marshal. None of these people had any type of experience. But those are the three people that were consistently showing the plan four times a week.

Obviously, I sponsored quite a few people and in order to identify those three particular people that really stepped up to the plate and decided to do what I was doing ...Was I discouraged? Did I ask myself how come all these other people are not doing it? Sometimes, but I did not dwell on that thought and I replaced it with a positive one and focused energy on what was actually working. Some people would continue to bail on me after beginning. All they were doing was using the given product and quitting. But why would I choose to be upset? Remember, *you become what you think about*. Whatever you focus on expands. If you're focusing on the three that are there, who are doing what you're doing, and that part expands, rather than focusing on the people that are not doing anything, then everything will expand.

You have to understand that if you do focus on the people that are not doing anything, that is the direction your energy and time will center on and you will not see positive results. This is a practical way of using the information I discussed earlier. It is very powerful!

Sometimes you must look back and think, "Did I do anything special to be successful in this business of network marketing?" Everything that you're reading right now, you've seen it before. You've learned about PBRs, you've learned about three-way calls, you've heard about prospecting. You've been exposed to all of the information. But it's that mental block in your mind of what it is that is coming out of your mouth in speaking. I do very little training on the base of the business because we have a system in place that trains people on the base of the business. I focus on training the mind ... really how the mindset works, how you can actually set your mind on fire. Tune your attention, just as you would tune a radio, to the place in your mind where the feeling of having money and success resides. Even if you say out loud, "Well I've never had money or success before," it doesn't matter. In your mind, imagine the exact feeling you would have if you checked your bank account and saw the amount of money you wished to have. Imagine the feeling of friends and family congratulating you on your success. Hear their voices in your head telling your what you want to hear. That's how you do it. If you can experience hearing someone's voice, then you can mentally give yourself the experience of hearing them say something congratulatory. It will become second nature. You will begin to see changes because once you train yourself to tune into the feeling of what you want to be subconsiously, you will naturally match your conscious life to it. Your subconsious knows no bounds and does not judge you. Your subconscious only knows what you feed it.

I can teach you how to do all these technical things, but if you don't have the belief system behind it, it's just not going to work. It is absolutely imperative that everyone understand this, because everything that you hear, you've heard it before—but if a person doesn't have the right belief system behind it, it's just not going to work. To me, what's interesting is than many people might think, "These are the things I wish you had written about in the first place." People tend to think, "Just give me the technical stuff. Tell me what to do and then I'll be all set." But I gave the information to you in this order for a reason.

It's interesting that you can share the information with people and explain exactly what to do but they still won't do it. This used to bother me so much. I would see people come to events and they would be pumped up. Then they would leave that event and do nothing. Do you know why? Because they went back to the same environment. They went back to the same people that were telling them that they couldn't do it. They went back to the same experiences. They went back to the same information. They didn't change their environment, they didn't change their experience, and they didn't change their *thinking*.

I heard many things in my time working this business. I heard faith, I heard believing, I didn't want to *hear* that. I wanted to be *shown*. Tell me what I need to do. *Show* me how to do a three-way call. Show me how to do a presentation. All those things are important. But all those things can be learned just by practice. Yet, how can I be certain … because everybody knows how to go about beginning and how do I make sure that this now works for me to get to the multi-million-dollar status? I don't just mean the $100,000 a year bracket. I'm talking about the quantum leap from where you are now. I'm talking about paradigm shifts—the things that you're saying all the time. Even as you're reading this book, you're probably saying, "I've heard this before."

That is hurting you, because you have not heard this before. You've never heard me talk before. And even if you have, have you really heard me? Have you really heard me on an audio? No. You haven't heard me through your car. So, you haven't heard me before. This is new and now you have to take the information and say, "Now I'm ready to go to the next level by writing this information down, seeing it every single day and then celebrating!" Celebrating. You hear it all the time, praise proceeds victory. You've got to celebrate it before it actually happens. The basis of the business is so simple. All I've done every single day for the last seven years is talked to two to five people per day. That's it. And people listen to those numbers and it doesn't really sound like a lot of numbers but for seven years, I've spoken to five people per day. Logically, they think, "I could do that." What tends to happen is they may start and they may do it for a day or two, or maybe even a week or two—and then all of a sudden they think, "I don't have to do it today. I've got this other thing going on." You must create consistency with this!

For many people it may not be easy. It's because of those concepts there that they deserve to listen to over and over again. When I say I talk to two to five people a day, what do I mean when I say that? What do you mean when you say you talk to two to five people a day? What constitutes talking to one person?

I'm basically exposing them to the opportunity. I'm meeting them and letting them know my name. I let them know what it is that I do.

When I meet a person, I'm not immediately going straight into the business. I'm going to build a rapport with this new person. I'm going to have a conversation with this person because I want to care about this person. If I'm going to spend time working with someone, I want to know that they need this opportunity or want this opportunity. I want to know a little bit about that person, and I want that person to know me, too. I always try to compliment people, that's a good way of starting off on the right foot with someone. But prospecting is just as much about confidence. I remember prospecting and people giving me the wrong number. I remember prospecting and people just walking away from me. I literally mean I was talking to them and they just walked away as if I was not even there. I would want to go home and cry to my dad and say, "This is not working." But immediately when that would happen, I would talk to the next person because you *have to fight fear.* Most people have a fear of talking to people. But the question you've got to ask yourself is this—Is the fear of talking to people stronger than the fear of being poor? Which one do you want? That's where that desire comes in.

I'm going to talk to whoever it is I can talk to because I know that it is a numbers game. It's the law of numbers. I heard Jim Rohn explain that in sowing those seeds, some are going to fall on rocky ground, some are going to fall on thorny ground, but some are going to fall on *your* ground. Finally, the seed falls on good ground. (It always will if you keep sowing.) I heard that and agreed, and eventually it will!

My mentor said that it's interesting because Jim Rohn and a lot of the things we are talking about are on his *Insider's Secrets to Making a Fortune*. When you're talking about listening to these people and listening to their messages and listening to what they're saying, you're talking about this same story and telling people what it means to talk to people. Some people get up close to someone and they start shaking or start convulsing or whatever the case may be. Some people really had a problem with talking to people but overcame that or transformed that. Maybe some people think that that never was the case for me. David just walked out of the womb and he was able to talk to people without a problem. If you don' t have a story with regard to yourself, with you really going through a serious challenge in even talking to people, tell us about someone that you know that's on your team, because you've got tens of thousands of people on your team that went through that as well but transformed. The point is that it is imperative to share that aspect—that there are obstacles like learning how to talk to people—and even if you didn't personally go through that, it is important to note who has gone through an experience like that.

One of the things that we teach to everybody is that it all goes back to the simplicity of what it is that you're doing. You've got to make sure that whatever it is that you're doing, a dud could actually talk to a stud about it. That's key. Because if you have something that's extremely difficult to talk about, then you need a superstar that's going to be able to explain it. Does that make sense? The fear of talking to people must be faced. You can even go up to a person and say, "You know what, I was actually not going to talk to you about this opportunity, but I don't want you to miss out on it because of my fear."

If you're talking to the right person, they're going to be moved simply by that statement that you made. That inner voice—the one that pushes you, motivates you and helps you and that tells you go talk to that person—that's really *you* talking. That's the champion inside of you telling you that the person you're talking to is going to allow you to be successful. When you don't listen to that voice, that voice stops talking to you. Whenever you hear that inner voice, you've got to make sure you take action. Don't worry about whether the person says yes or no. What do you have to lose? You have absolutely nothing to lose. I tell people all the time, "Believing costs you nothing. Doubting costs you everything."

My goal in the very beginning was to

sponsor two to four people per month by talking to two to five people a day. So let's take three people for a thought experiment. If you work the system in talking to three people for three times, thirty days in the month, then you've got 90 people that you're talking to. So you if you get two or three people started then hey, that's great!

Here's the beauty of this: the two people per day is not for you. The two people per day is for duplication purposes. Let's say I talk to two people per day for five days per week. So that's 10 people for the week, multiplied by four will equal 40 people. Well what if I teach two other people to do it with me? Now I've got 80 plus my 40, that's 120 people per month finding out about who's business?—my business. What if I taught it to 10 people? That's 20 per day, times 5. That's 100 times 4, that's 400. One out of 10. If we went to one out of 10, that's 40 people joining our business that month—if we only got one out of 10. But what did we learn before? That every time you do something, a ratio appears. Then if you do it enough times, the ratio improves. You may start off as one out of 10. But as you continue to train and continue to go to events and continue to work on your belief system, it can grow to two out of 10. What if you get to three out of 10? Now we're talking about four million dollars a year.

When I first began, it was one out of 30. At least I had a ratio. That's the key, you've got to get a ratio and the only way you're going to get that is to talk to enough people to make that happen. So, these three people that I originally began with started to duplicate me and began replicating what I was doing. As I have mentioned, one was postal worker, one was a teacher, another a federal marshal. These people did not have dramatic and successful results in network marketing before. I know one individual was involved in another company for nine months. She made $1,600 in nine months, total. She was a $1,600 earner. Another had 81 people in his business in two years. So no, no success whatsoever. But because of a system and consistency they kept working, they kept believing.

Here is the key thing: if you're going to get to that next level, you're going to have to become magnetic enough to really attract the people who are going to come in and take you to the next level.

The person I was four years ago couldn't have attracted a conversation with a person like my mentor. Therefore I had to develop myself in order to be able to attract what is happening in my life right now. After doing the work from the standpoint of building my beliefs and doing the work of actually talking to two to five people per day along with doing the presentations for one person, sometimes for no people, or for three people, and showing up when nobody else was showing up, things changed. Going to the weekly meeting, week after week, month after month going to those trainings, going to those events, I became attractive enough to bring in some people that had experience in the industry. That's where the Solace King came into the business. That's where the hard hitters came into business. Those individuals now came into the business and I'm thinking, "These people have more experience than me. They actually had made more money than me in the industry." But because I had worked so hard on my craft, they now looked at me and said, "I want to do business with that young man!"

People that I have talked to about the business two years ago, two and a half years ago … they always keep the following in mind: I just had a gentleman who just got started. I talked to him two and a half years ago. But he said "no" to the person I was two and a hal years ago. If you're reading this book, I want you to remember this. If you don't get anything out of this, I'm talking about building your business. Remember this: The people that are telling you "no" today—they are saying "no" to the person that you are today ... not the person that you're going to be six months from now. The person that you're going to be six months from now or two years from now will not be the person they say "no" to. They are going to say, "Yes, please put me in, I'm ready. I'm ready to work with you." That's what's happening today. People that would laugh at me two and a half years ago are now calling me and saying, "Hey, I heard good things about what you're doing. Can you please put me in the system?" Remember, if I didn't stay consistent, if I didn't keep reading those books and listening to those recordings and learning to change my thoughts and getting the signs it may not have happened ... He said he would confirm His Word with signs and wonders. So the words that I write down, they're going to be confirmed by the signs that I put up and the wonders revealed. I have my sign.

The wonder is you becoming a multimillionaire, you becoming a success. But what do you do with that and the reality of time? Are you patient? Are you continuously working? Are you continuously staying inspired by going to those events and listening to those recordings and those CDs? Being dedicated, being disciplined is key. I know this works. I'm explaining this to you because I've been quite successsful with it since my late twenties. I know what works. This works. I spent seven years in this industry working on success with four and a half years of failing. Then I surpassed three years of absolute success. It was not an overnight success. It took seven years! Is it worth it? Is it worth it for you to stay on track for seven years and wake up seven years later as a multimillionaire? I don't care how old you are. If you are reading this book right now you need to understand that it works. Believing works. It works, but you've got to put the work behind it.

The PS3

If you start off with conceiving, you believe and you achieve. There are many other points. But the main key for people to grasp is the *understanding*. We want to give them some of the technical information that they really want. The main message that people need to understand is that they already know the technical side, really. It's just a matter of allowing yourself to go out and execute it. You must allow yourself to do it and that's only going to happen if you have a powerful enough vision that will propel you forward—even when things are not going well right away. But you must allow yourself to keep focusing on what it is you desire instead of what it is you *don't* desire.

Do you have a heart for people? Be honest about this ... that must be the question you've got to ask yourself. If you read this book and you're part of network marketing, you've got to ask yourself, "Do I have a heart for people?" Because if you have a heart for people, you'll never quit. No matter what you're going through, you'll never quit. You won't quite because you know there's somebody out there that you need to talk to. *So, do you have a heart for people?* I had a heart for people. Today, I still have a heart to be able to see people win and that's what keeps me going. What's going to keep you going? Because success is not going to happen right away, and when it does happen, guess what? There's still another level to attain. That's really important for people to understand.

Many people reading this may not have earned $5,000 a month yet in network marketing and they may figure, "I'll get to $5,000 and month and that's going to be great." Or maybe they figure that's not the end at all, they probably already know that at $5,000 a month. But then they get to $5,000 and say, "I'm going to get to $10,000 and they get to $10,000 and they say, "Once I get to $20,000, I'm going to really set myself up. And they get there and maybe they get to $30,000 and they say to themselves, "Once I get to $30,000, I'm set. Once you get to the $30,000 mark, you might ask yourself, "What am I going to do with this?" Then you might set your sights at $100,000 a month and say, "Once I get to $100,000 a month, I know there can't be much beyond that." But then you reach $100,000 a month and realize things are nicer—things are great!

The only reason why I kept developing myself was because of Mr. Buggs. The only reason why I kept growing was because of some of the top leaders with whom I had worked. These guys kept moving up, so my comfort zone also shifted along with theirs ... I could not stay comfortable at six figures a month. Why? Because I was around people that would be making multiple six figures, touching on seven figures a month. Therefore it falls back to the environment in which you surround yourself. Your environment and what you hear and see is what is going to impact you the most. It's what will make you say, "I want to do more."

However, on the flip side of that same coin, a major issue can occur. If you are the big fish in the pond, you might not have the motivation to keep growing. So the people that are following you are important, but the people that you're following are even *more* important.

Before I come to a close, I really want to explore the concept of how to move from where it is that you are right now to now and taking some practical steps. I want to explore the questions like: What do I need to do after reading this book? The very first thing I would recommend a person to do is get their hands on some personal self-development. You've got to get your hands on that type of material right away. It's why I dedicated so much of this book to writing about it. You must make sure that you're listening to it every single moment of the day. You've got to drown yourself in the right words because words create everything. The words that I've been listening to create my life.

I want to change my life, I've got to now change the words that I'm listening to. I may not know the right words to speak right now, but there is somebody else out there that needs to get motivational tapes. They need to get the things that have been put out there. Then they can get and understand this is what they need to be downloading not only onto their phone to listed to throughout the day but also into their subconscious. If I'm thinking of what I need to listen to in order to feed my mind the words I need, I know that I need to download *Magic of Believing*. I need to download *The Strangest Secret*. I need to download the Jim Rohn recordings. I need to download all of these in order to extract the information that has been coming in.

Set a daily goal of what you're going to do in your business. An example of daily goals are as follows: How many people am I going to talk to per day? Two to five people per day. That's a very simple goal to achieve. How many presentations am I going to do per day? Am I going to show the plan one time today? How often am I going to communicate with my coach or my mentor? These are some practical things that you can do right now to move from where you currently are to the next level.

Definitely stick with what your coaches are teaching you. There are so many different systems out there and they all work. It's not one system, one book, one tape, one mentor that's going to allow you to actually get to the next level. They will assist you, but they won't carve out a path of certainty for you to get to the next level. The only thing that's going to allow you to do that are the words that you let into your life right now ... the *correct* information.

Everything that you've read in this book hasn't come from me. It's a culmination of information that's been downloaded for the last seven years that I've put together for a comprehensive understanding. You've got to make sure you put yourself through the process of listening and *believing*. Remember, all things are possible to those that believe. So learn how to believe. Learn how to put yourself in the right environment. Learn how to experience the things that will benefit you the most. Learn how to be around the right people. Learn how to speak the right words, how to see the right things and how to experience the right emotions ... these all must align with your personal vision. You cannot let words, emotions, people or your environment stifle your belief.

Every now and then, I decide to celebrate in my house. I just scream and yell and let myself get excited for no particular reason. When I look at the word excited—*cited* means proof, *ex* means my past. When I'm excited, I'm basically looking at something—proof of something—and I'm putting it in my past. So, you can get excited right now where you are sitting. You can get excited about a six figure a month income. Just because it is not here today in your account doesn't mean you can't get excited and experience the same feeling you would have if you saw the proof and you knew it came from your past. You can get excited about it. And those emotions are what will drive you even closer to getting to that six figure per month income. I heard it on an audio. The quantum leap of 3% to 97% and what the difference is between people that make six figures a year versus the people that make six figures per month. It's just the paradigms!

That original audio I recorded a long time ago in order to listen to it repeatedly made a huge impact in my life. Once again, it was the power of information. If I had never heard that information, where would I be today?

Everything that I'm sharing with you creates some sort of impact. Everything you do every day creates some sort of impact, whether it's today or further down the line when it manifests. We may all be surprised at the impact that we don't know now and we probably will never know. It may be 10 years from now that someone will say, "Hey David, I read this book and you wrote something in there that made a difference to me. There were a couple of things in there that you gave me. The action steps and that revolutionized my life. You know we were talking about Jim Rohn and this book, and Clark Bristol and Earl Nightingale". Someday somebody is going to be saying that about you and about me. And that's the power of what we can do as being a part of this industry and being a part of this business.

One of the things that I heard on that audio *Think and Win Big* was that impact drives income. It's all about how many lives you can impact. I've got a good friend of mine who just got started with this and that's what we talk about all the time. How many people can we impact? How many lives can we change? Somebody may be reading this book that may have even thought of quitting. They may have thought of letting their goals and their dreams fade away, and because they read this book they are going to press on one more day. I want them to understand that that's success. Success is doing it one more time—doing one more three-way call, doing one more PBR, going to one more event. That's success. Success is a progressive realization of a worthy ideal. It is a moving target. You never actually reach success, so why be frustrated if it hasn't happened yet? You never reach it. Because when you get there, there's always something else. There's another level to attain. I want you to understand that. There's always another level and the way that you're going to get to that level is to make sure you *conceive* your desire, make sure you *believe* in it and yourself and you will *achieve* everything you want. You will achieve that next level you want to reach. You will achieve what it is that you are seeking to accomplish. Find an audio that resonates with you and listen to it over and over and over again maybe for months at a time like I did—it's absolutely amazing what it will do for your mentality.

Go back and review this information over and over again. Find the parts that really speak to you and underline them. *Think* on them. *Visualize* what you want—you've got to be able to know what you want—and see yourself as already having it. As one of my mentors says, "Keep charging and always remember to ... hold on, and go, go, go!